Tay Bridge On the night of Sunday December 28, 1879, the unthinkable happened. Battered by a ferocious storm, the Tay Bridge collapsed. *Tay Bridge* tells the poignant and unexpected stories of the suddenly interrupted passengers making the journey that night. Who were they? Where were they going? A powerful ensemble piece, *Tay Bridge* gives a whole new perspective on this famous bridge disaster.

The Signalman Winter 1919. Thomas Barclay is transported back in time by his memories of the night when he was the Signalman who sent the Edinburgh/Burntisland train onto the Tay Rail Bridge forty years before. Who is responsible when accidents occur? Why do we need somebody to blame…even if it's ourselves?

T0131235

Peter Arnott

TWO PLAYS

Tay Bridge & The Signalman

Salamander Street

PLAYS

First published in 2019 by Salamander Street Ltd.

Printed and bound in Great Britain

10 9 8 7 6 5 4 3 2 1

CONTENTS

Contents

Playwright's Note

Sometimes you don't end up exactly where you thought you were going. Sometimes your actual destination is better. Even if it does involve a dive into the freezing waters of the Tay.

Tay Bridge and *The Signalman* both had their origins in conversations while working some years ago with an actor called Tom McGovern, who was inspired by a Thornton Wilder novel called *The Bridge of San Luis Rey* to look again at the story of the Tay Bridge Disaster…but not at the incompetence and possible corruption which led to the disaster, but from the viewpoint of people aboard the train who have no idea what is about to happen to them. What lives were interrupted by the accident? What journeys were never completed?

I loved the idea. There was something inherently theatrical, I thought, in EVERYONE in the audience knowing that a disaster is coming, but the characters on stage knowing nothing. I came up with the idea that Tom would play the Signalman Thomas Barclay who sent the train onto the Bridge…haunted ever since…and that the play would also feature those accidental passengers.

And like most ideas, it got filed away under 'One of these Days'.

Cut to a conversation a year and a bit ago with Andrew Panton, the director of Dundee Rep, who said he wanted a show specially written to celebrate the 20th anniversary of the Ensemble of actors who make Dundee Rep so unique in Scottish Theatre – written by someone who knew them all, tailoring the script to their particular and considerable skills.

And what had been an idea for one play became an idea to create two shows…one for the very special circumstances of Dundee Rep's Birthday Celebrations – the show marked the 80th birthday of the company as well as the 20th anniversary of the Ensemble as a collective – and the other tailored to Tom McGovern's extraordinary inventiveness and intensity as an actor, facilitated through the good offices of Glasgow Lunchtime Theatre at Òran Mór.

I began exploring historical sources, reliable and unreliable…and found that stories, true or not, about the passengers and crew, had emerged almost at the moment their bodies began to rise out of the silt where they had fallen. The most moving of these records is the bald statement of their names and dress and possessions assembled by the Tay Valley Family History Society. I would also draw on the testimony given to the Official Enquiry by Thomas Barclay. I would match the real stories to the real actors as best I could…and fictionalise the rest in the two scripts published together here.

At Dundee Rep, well as the actors, Andrew Panton assembled quite a team to tell their stories. Composer MJ McCarthy, Lighting Designer Simon Wilkinson, animations director Lewis Den Hertog and designer Emily James. As for Tom McGovern, he and I were very fortunate to get the assured and inspired support of Ken Alexander as director for the solo show at Glasgow Lunchtime Theatre.

The writing of these stories has meant an entrance into the mental world of Scotland a hundred and forty years ago…and an exploration of memory and what memory means. That has been a journey in itself. But it is the unexpected journey to become part of what I hope are two strong and deceptively ambitious theatrical experiences that wasn't quite the journey I anticipated making…and which I'm especially glad and pleasantly surprised that I made.

Peter Arnott, September 2019

Tay Bridge

Tay Bridge was first performed on Tuesday 27 August 2019 at Dundee Rep. It was written by Peter Arnott from an original idea by Tom McGovern.

The cast was Leah Byrne, Ewan Donald, Barrie Hunter,
Anne Kidd, Irene MacDougall, Bailey Newsome
and Emily Winter.

Director Andrew Panton
Designer Emily James
Composer/Sound Designer Michael John McCarthy
Lighting Designer Simon Wilkinson
Movement Director Emily-Jane Boyle
AV Designer Lewis Den Hertog

OVERTURE the underwater world

Swirling, turbulence. A chaos of images and music. Lines from the stories we are about to see and hear, snatches of song…are mixed with a musical theme and the sounds of water, weather…and disaster. As the picture forms of our characters standing on the remains of the pillar supports of the first Tay Rail Bridge that still jut eerily from the shallow waters of the Firth, we hear and see them more distinctly, more individually. **NEISH**, *a schoolteacher wearing a black armband of mourning;* **MRS EASTON**, *the widow of a clergyman and aspiring author;* **ANNIE CRUIKSHANK, A HOUSEKEEPER** *and* **SERVANT; BENYON**, *a travelling* **SALESMAN; EMILY**, *a kept woman and actress;* **ELIZA**, *a young servant and her fiancé,* **GEORGE JOHNSTONE**, *a mechanic.*

NEISH Tis not in mere mortals to command success. We will do more. We will deserve it!

MRS EASTON *(Holding her manuscript.)* How can I present this to the world now? What can it be worth now? How dare I tell the story of my life when it turns out I knew nothing about it?

ANNIE CRUIKSHANK Aren't I your freen? Aren't I the only one who was always here?

BENYON I keep thinking that somebody's going to stop me. But nobody does. Nobody ever sees me for what I am.

ELIZA *(To* **GEORGE**.*)* George Johnstone! I am telling you now, you are going to need tae tell me what you want or you and me are finished!

EMILY God will find a way to punish me. One day. I know He will.

The music crashes. We see the moment of the disaster (in reverse?) as experienced by our first story teller – the school teacher **DAVID NEISH**. *The train is re-arranged for Neish's story. Once the carriage is reconstructed,* **NEISH** *tells his story to the other passengers…who through long practice, are now participants as well as audience. As his story progresses, the set is minimally altered to aid his story telling, which is also aurally supported by music and sound design.*

MR NEISH'S STORY

NEISH Failure is the best discipline. That's what Mr Durisdeer taught me. I can still hear him.

(In the voice of his dead teacher.)

'Failure, my dear boys, if only it is joined by perseverance, is full of instruction. Tis not in mere mortals to *command* success. We will do more. We will *deserve* it!'

(In his own voice.)

We will deserve it.

(He begins the catechism.)

Who made you?

PASSENGERS as **CHILDREN** *(Knowing the story, joining in.)* God, Mr Neish!

NEISH What else did God make?

CHILDREN God made all things, Mr Neish.

NEISH Why did God make you and all things?

CHILDREN For his own glory, Mr Neish.

NEISH How can you and I glorify God?

CHILDREN By loving him and doing what he commands, Mr Neish.

NEISH By loving him and doing what he commands.

His commandment is simple. Isn't it? His commandment is tae dae right. And aabiddy kens whit's right. Aabiddy. We aa ken when we dae right...and we surely ken it fine when we dae wrang.

Since I began teaching, I've been doing what Mr Durisdeer taught me. I've been looking for faces amang aa the other faces. And I dae see them. If only for a term...a month...a week...faces ae a certain... quality...

What quality is that?

Weel...no like they were characters in a book...lost aristocrats mistakenly placed amang the rabble.

It's sadness...I think. Sadness for the world. Is that fanciful?

Very well. It's fanciful.

MCQUARRIE Has Oliver Twist appeared yet in yer classroom, Mr Neish? Or Becky Sharp?

NEISH I fear not, Mr McQuarrie.

MCQUARRIE Will you let us all know when they reveal themselves… so we can all come and stare at them…in wonder.

*(Passengers laugh, joining in **MCQUARRIE***'s cynicism.)*

NEISH *(Silencing them.)* Why is it sae easy…to mock? Why is it easier to despair than to hope? Because it is merr comfortable tae surrender to a bad world than tae strive for a better yin. One looks sophisticatit, when one is, in fact, craven. One appears realistic when one is, in fact, self-serving.

In any case, I found him. I saw his face. His singular face amang aa the ither faces. Euan MacBride. I spoke tae him. I found something in him. I saw…a spark…

And I needed a colleague to support me in my argument to the headmaister that this pupil of outstanding promise merited individual tuition…and transfer tae a merr advanced class…and there was naebiddy else on the staff I thocht would support me. So I asked McQuarrie. Looking back, asking help from that man was the very worst thing I could have done.

*(Bar lighting and ambience. **NEISH** steps forward into a reconstructed memory. The **ELIZA** actress plays the barmaid from his own 'compartment')*

I'm not used to coming into a place like this. What if one of the elders should see us?

MCQUARRIE To see us, they'd need to be in here themselves. And then we'd see them. Heavens, you've a lot to learn about school teaching!

BARMAID What will ye tak, Mister McQuarrie?

MCQUARRIE Whisky, my pet. As ever.

BARMAID And your pal? Ur ye new here?

NEISH Water. Thank ye.

BARMAID *(Serving* **MCQUARRIE**.*)* You a domine n'a'?

NEISH Yes.

BARMAID *(Indicates* **MCQUARRIE**.*)* But no like this yin, eh?

MCQUARRIE *(Hugging her, enjoying* **NEISH***'s discomfort.)* Elsa here was one of my pupils. Weren't you, sweetheart? Before your time, Mr Neish.

    *(***BARMAID** *gets* **NEISH***'s water)*

NEISH Thank you.

MCQUARRIE *(To* **ELSA**.*)* Polite, isn't he?

    (She laughs and leaves.)

Well, speak up, Mr Neish! We've only half an hour for luncheon.

NEISH We should we put Euan MacBride in the scholarship class. I can prepare him.

MCQUARRIE Have we any reason to think he will have the active support of his family?

NEISH I have spoken to his mother. She wants the best for him.

MCQUARRIE She does not provide him with shoes.

NEISH I can provide his footwear. If we but elevate him to the place where he has a chance…he will take that chance. And we will be proud of him. The whole school will be proud.

MCQUARRIE Or embarrassed. This is a dangerous game you're playing, Mr Neish. The governors know of your wee projects…and they know that the prospect exists of being made fools of. They care about these things. They go to dinner with men they should prefer did not laugh at them behind their napkins.

    (Classroom ambience.)

NEISH Why ought you to glorify God?

CHILDREN Because he made me and takes care of me, Mr Neish.

NEISH Are there more gods than one?

CHILDREN There is only one God, Mr Neish.

NEISH Only one God…one truth. One truth to learn.

(Bar room ambience.)

MCQUARRIE Learn? Sixty unhappy brats in a single cold classroom, all ages, all abilities! They cannot learn in an Artisan School as they understand the word at the University. One can thrash some rudimentary repetitions into them! But teach? Hardly! And why teach them anything at all if they can only learn to despise their lot in life? When they can be contented, ignorant servants in agriculture, industry and domestic service!

NEISH Euan is not going to be a servant! That is why…

MCQUARRIE Some may end in prison or the army, and a little beating from us will accustom them to that life too. And for the rest, let us pass the time for them and for ourselves as pleasantly as maybe.

NEISH If they are fated to bleach and spin and weave, it is an accident of history and geography. But is it not true that every advance in human history has come from those who broke the bounds of necessity? Should we not take account of the exceptional?

MCQUARRIE You? For example…

NEISH Me? We're not talking about me…

MCQUARRIE Are we not, though? Farmtoun boy made good? Durisdeer…was that not yer teacher's name?

NEISH We are talking about *our* pupil. Euan MacBride.

MCQUARRIE If you say so…

NEISH He is of exceptional ability and intelligence, you can see that. But unless he has help from you and me, then yes…it may be his destiny to submit to a working life of severity and poverty…but more likely, given his energy and intelligence, crime…a life of crime…

MCQUARRIE Are we saving our citizens from a master criminal now?

NEISH *becomes uncomfortably aware of their conversation being listened to, and that the listeners think he's being naïve.*

NEISH We are intervening in the life of a single child…a single child who stands for many…whose lives are dictated to them from slum

7

childhood to slum solitude and death as absolutely as if they were subjects of any Satrap.

MCQUARRIE *(To the enjoyment of the listeners.)* Control yourself, Mr Neish! Satraps and master criminals, is it? He seems a soulful wee chap to me…especially given the family of Neanderthals he springs from…

NEISH *(Insisting against the crowd.)* Should we not try to do right by him?

MCQUARRIE Do right? Possibly! The price for my assistance is the truth.

NEISH The truth?

MCQUARRIE Are you sure…when you think of young Master MacBride …that you're not thinking of yourself at a similar age… plucked from similar obscurity by your own village domine? Up from rural ignorance to the University of Dundee. Years of struggle, study…of learning the manners and voices of a gentleman!

NEISH Aye. Mainners you were born wi…raised wi…I had to claw them oot ae the earth…

MCQUARRIE Like potatoes! And yet here we are…colleagues. You raised from your rural idiocy to the dizzy heights of a parochial schoolteacher…and me fallen from on high to exactly the same status. That you are here with me is testament to your years of industry…That I am here with you…is testament to my indolence and failure. Which of us is more poisoned with frustrated ambition? Me or you?

NEISH Will you help me with Euan MacBride? Will you support me with the headmaster? No matter what you think my motivations are?

MCQUARRIE You must not teach him to fly higher than his wings are made for. I hope you'll not regret your ambition, like Daedalus… watching your Icarus fall into the Tay…

(The listeners laugh. **NEISH** *silences them with the catechism.)*

NEISH Does God know all things?

CHILDREN Yes; nothing can be hid from God, Mr Neish.

NEISH Nothing can be hid from God!

(Confessing, his hand touching his black armband.)

All right. It's true. Without Mr Durisdeer, I would never have been ambitious. I would never have fallen into …this hatred…and disappointment.

(Euan steps forward to sit at a desk for solo instruction.)

But Euan MacBride…a faither lost at sea…a mither subsisting on charity…his family living in a single room with another family similarly indigent…against all odds, all expectation…he has a spark of…possibility. He has not an ounce of privilege…but merr ability…merr promise than I ever had.

Perhaps his best outcome will be as paltry as ma ain…But wi'oot my help…whatever hope he has will come to nothing. And whatever God in his heaven knows of me and my motivation…it is still the right thing to do.

One child at a time. We can save the world one child at a time.

(As he recites, the passengers slowly join in, as they did in the catechism.)

Amo, Amas, Amat. Amamis, Amatis, Amant.

I love, you love, he loves, we love. You love, they love

Discam Disces Discet Discemus Disceti Discent

I will learn, you will learn, he will learn, we will learn, you will learn…they will learn.

We will deserve it.

PASSENGERS We will deserve it.

(He has his audience listening to him now. Reaching the climax of his story.)

It took a year. A year of tuition and expense to myself…but Euan was ready…and on Friday morning a week ago, I closed off and heated a room for him to come and sit the scholarship exam…I had paid his entrance fee as the governors of the school would not…I had taken a day off work…officially…I had brought Professor Taft of the University…my old tutor… to conduct the examination in person. Latin. History. Geography. Theology and Moral Thought.

And we sat together. The Professor and I. As Nine O'Clock struck…
as a minute went by…two minutes….five….and an awful certainty
afflicted me…

(He hurries to ask at the school office.)

I went, I asked, and I discovered what I should have known. Euan
had not come to school that morning. Yesterday, in the last lesson
of the day. McQuarrie had beaten him. Beaten him savagely like a
slave. Today…Euan had not come to school. God knows if he would
ever come back.

I'd lost him.

I was stunned…staggered…and without forethought, I found myself
in McQuarrie's class room…where he was teaching the catechism.

*(The children/listeners are now hostile to **MCQUARRIE**.)*

MCQUARRIE What did God give Adam and Eve besides bodies?

CHILDREN He gave them souls that could never die, Mister
McQuarrie.

MCQUARRIE Have you a soul as well as a body?

CHILDREN Yes; I have a soul that can never die, Mr McQuarrie

MCQUARRIE *(Grins.)* Can I help you, Mr Neish?

*(**NEISH** strikes him. Uproar. We return to the train. **NEISH** addresses
his fellow passengers.)*

NEISH I lost my job. Of course I did. But by begging favours, perhaps
I'll find a position in some country school, the kind of school I went
to. Where Mr Durisdeer taught me.

He died last week in his classroom. It took the last of my savings to
bury him. He died of the work he had done all his life.

Tomorrow will be different. Tomorrow will be better.

We will deserve it.

*(Transition. Music. **MRS EASTON** is the next story teller so it is her
experience of the disaster that we see…and to her story that we return. Train
ambience.)*

MRS EASTON'S STORY

MRS EASTON *(Sits looking at her manuscript. To her fellow passengers.)* I wish I could read to you from my manuscript. But the illumination from the paraffin lamps is as questionable as the insulation! I do know the beginning by heart. I begin the story of my life with this 'Perhaps my husband was not a bad man, but taking him at his own estimation, I found myself so far below him, that I had no choice but to hate him, just a little.' I do think that's rather good!

> *The passengers, performing from her manuscript – of which they have all found pages in the silt, now as her husbands' congregants, sing a hymn. Church sound picture.*

REVEREND EASTON We complain, don't we? We complain about everything. On and on and on. But let us reflect, dear friends, that as adherents of the Church of Scotland, we are blessed! Our missionaries bring our Presbyterian light to the darkness of the world! As the most dynamic servants of the British Empire, we Scots are the Chosen People of Today every bit as much as were the Children of Israel in the days of Gideon!

MRS EASTON *(To the passengers.)* That's what he was like. That's the kind of thing he said in the pulpit every Sunday. And was my husband not the expert in the workings of divine providence, having married my father's money when he married me!

> *(Light fades on the **REVEREND EASTON**.)*

When my husband had his living in the city, when I still believed I loved him, or at least that I ought to try, our parish included what was called the Holy Land, a place whose name derived from the strange presence in Whitehall Close of the most haunting and primitive carving on a wall...showing Adam and Eve...in paradise.

Paradise. Good God.

> *(**THE REVEREND**, in her memory, approaches her. He is accompanied by a young and intense medical inspector, **DR COOPER**.)*

REVEREND EASTON It is my duty, my dear, to accompany Dr Cooper on his demonstrative excursion to the dwellings of the poor. But it is none of yours.

MRS EASTON *(Narrating in the present.)* I insisted on coming along. Perhaps I was curious to see how the poor lived. But I had already heard so much from that intense young man…and Dr Cooper…God forgive me… that young man was so compelling! And I was young, then, too!

(In her memory, the tour begins. She joins them as **COOPER** *speaks.)*

COOPER If there were one thing that would do more than any other to transform life in this city…it is water!

(Street sounds. They stand in a dark entrance way.)

MRS EASTON *(In the moment, in the past.)* Water! Such a simple thing and in such plentiful supply in these latitudes. One would have thought.

(Laughs.)

COOPER *(Humourless.)* A water supply tae meet the needs ae hygiene in the lower town would revolutionise hundreds of lives in this street alone, Mrs Easton. With water, their chances of decency, of virtue, of rising above animality, exist. Without it, they do not.

REVEREND EASTON The cost to the city, Dr Cooper, would be prohibitive.

COOPER What is the cost of not trying, Reverend? What is the cost to these folk of existing as they do? What is the cost to our souls of blinking at their misery?

(He gestures that they enter the darkness…they do…shadows overwhelm them… **COOPER** *lights a lamp.)*

MRS EASTON It was like walking into the mouth of hell as we stepped into the close…one's eyes stung…watering at the devil's breath. I had to steel myself, recover my balance…lean against a wall dripping with the condensing perspiration of all the souls within.

(In live action, **MRS EASTON** *reacts to the smell.)*

Oh!

(Then narrating.)

The smell...I'm sorry...but it's what I most remember. It got into my nostrils and has never left them. I can smell it even now. Nothing smells as bad as poverty.

(**COOPER** *continues 'live' as they climb stone stairs. Sound FX.*)

COOPER Thanks to the lobbying efforts of our property owning classes, the sanitary act of 1866 is only enforceable by application to English courts...whose writ stops at Carlisle.

MRS EASTON His voice went on as we ascended the stairs into the darkness.

(*Footsteps, sinister music.* **COOPER** *and the* **MINISTER** *ascend in a spiral...light opens to reveal Annie Cruickshank's compartment, now strewn with straw. Annioe Cruiksghank actor plays 'Woman.'* **NIESH** *actor plays 'Man.')*

COOPER How can one 'morally improve' a population who must stand for hours among depravity and drunkenness...merely to fetch water, a bucket of water filled from a broken pipe...one single illegal standpipe for a thousand, two thousand citizens.

(*They reach Journey's End...hung with a washing line. Straw on the floor.*)

Here. Reverend. Mrs Easton...In here.

MRS EASTON Fresh human filth was piled in old straw that furnished bedding as well as sanitation in this room where people slept... fifteen of them...Two families. Only three people were there that morning. There was a child, male or female, I couldn't tell...their hair was caked with...unspeakable...and the woman apologised to me for the distress I was being caused.

WOMAN I'm sorry. I'm sorry. What can ah dee?

(**MRS EASTON** *in the past is/was unable to reply...so retreats to story telling.*)

MRS EASTON In that wretched den on the upper storey, none the brighter or lighter for being nearer heaven, the husband had been 'down with fever' for six weeks. He was wandering, murmuring incessantly.

MAN (*In her memory, rather alarmingly, shocking her.*) I'm parched, Missus... I'm really thirsty.

(**WOMAN** *helps him drink.*)

MRS EASTON The child kept crawling into the filthy straw, so that between it and her husband the poor woman had not a moment's rest. On a line across the room a half-washed sheet was hanging, steaming as it dried.

WOMAN He's got bed-sores, and they run a good deal, and I'm such a weak body, I canna haul enuech water tae to wash him. He drinks near aa I bring.

MINISTER Can he not go out to work?

WOMAN He cannae work...we lost oor auld room...and syne we've came here I cannae get the water to keep him clean. I wis hauf an oor in the morn fetchin a pail ae water, and in the derk of the stair somebody ran intae me..and it was aa spilled.

MRS EASTON I'm so sorry.

(*She tries to comfort the woman, but both of them helpless.*)

Can't anything be done, Doctor Cooper?

COOPER Such it is to be slaves of water, Mrs Easton. Without it, how can one raise oneself even into elementary health or decency?

REVEREND EASTON (*Resentful of* **COOPER**'s *efforts to get at him through his wife.*) You have made your case, Dr Cooper...with the help of an ably coached witness. My wife and I are very moved. But I think we've seen enough.

MRS EASTON Pray don't make me the excuse...for leaving...

REVEREND EASTON (*To the woman, giving her a shilling.*)

Perhaps this will be a little help...

WOMAN Thank you, sir. God bless you!

(*The* **WOMAN** *kisses his hand.* **MRS EASTON** *is appalled. The* **REVEREND** *turns to his wife, wiping his hand.*)

I'm sorry you saw this, my dear. But the will of the Lord is mysterious. Such things are sent to try us.

MRS EASTON (*Narrating.*)

Why was he saying sorry to me? Why was he sorry at all and not angry...at people being forced to live like this?

(Furious, to her husband's 'shade'.)

It is not me before whom you should abase yourself. If is God you should say sorry to. You should be on your knees like a Catholic.

That's what I should have said to him. I said nothing of the sort. I said nothing.

*(The **REVEREND** returns to his pulpit, and preaches in the words of the Moderator of the Church of Scotland at the time.)*

REVEREND EASTON The remedy of poverty does not lie in the liberality of the rich; it lies in the hearts and habits of the poor. There is no help for them if they will not help themselves. It is to a rise and reformation in the habits of our paupers that we look to for deliverance, not to the impotent crudities of speculative legislation.

(We return to the train ambience. The other passengers listen closely.)

MRS EASTON *(With her manuscript back in her hand.)* Separation being of course, unthinkable, I turned inward to my reading, to my writing. Oh, I did my outward duties as a minister's wife... I governed my household and my servants with kindness, with decency...I hope. I gave of my weekly allowance to charity. When I would come to peer over the shoulder of my Maker at what was written against my name in the book of life, I still thought to find myself on the positive side of the ledger.

But I only felt alive when I wrote the lives of others, in my little room in our house at Broughty Ferry...my tales of country life, of redemption and forgiveness. I wrote them for myself...or so I told my late husband when I closed the door upon him...to sit at my desk, looking out over the firth, in fair weather and in foul.

(There is an ominous gust of wind. She refers to her manuscript.)

And then he died...my husband, and God forgive me...I felt able to be truthful, and at last, with this account of my own life ...I really thought I'd written something honest and worthwhile. Something for the ages, perhaps...

(She looks at her work. Smiles at the other passengers. Holds it to herself.)

I thought…when I went to Edinburgh on Friday last for the winding up of my husband's estate, I might even take it to a publisher there. After all, now I command my own wealth, reverted to me in the absence of a son, I can easily afford the costs of publication… and I can begin my life again. As an author!

But at the solicitors' office, I discovered, on proceeding with the winding up of my husband's estate, that the very slum in which we had found that child…that we had owned it. That my father…and then my husband through me…had owned it. We had lived off its rent, and that of a dozen other filthy warrens like it…And when it had been demolished as a hazard to public health…we had been generously compensated.

All my comforts…my wealth…But my education, too… even my secret story telling…had all proceeded from that misery. The food I ate, the house I lived in…all of it…

Oh, I'm a wealthy woman, now…and I can use my wealth to do good. I am free at last…but I can't forget…where my freedom came from.

(Looking at her manuscript.)

How can I present this to the world now? What can it be worth now? How dare I tell the story of my life when it turns out I knew nothing about it?

I should get up. I should get up now. I should stand up and open the window… and I should open my portfolio to the wild winds outside…lose my life in the storm and the darkness.

I won't, of course. Instead I will sit here quietly in the dark, as I always have…with my thoughts…Perhaps I'll know better what to do tomorrow.

(Transition. **ANNIE CRUICKSHANK** *is featured and established.)*

ANNIE CRUICKSHANK'S STORY

(ANNIE CRUICKSHANK, *a servant, is talking to other passengers, who are clearly sympathetic to her side of her story.)*

ANNIE CRUICKSHANK Good morning, madam. I says tae her. Like I says every morning. And whit does she say tae me? 'My faither never liked you.' That's what she says to me.

ELIZA Naw! She didna really say that!!

ANNIE CRUICKSHANK She did! Oot ae naewhere. Oot ae Naethin! The disrespect!

BENYON Dear dear! How distressing for you!

NEISH That doesn't seem right at aa.

ANNIE My faither never liked you! Where in the name of the wee man did that come fae?

ELIZA What did you dae? What did you say to her?

ANNIE CRUICKSHANK I was dumstoonert! I was ragin. I could feel masel gan reed in the mou'! You've changed yer tune, I said tae masel! That wasnae how it wis atween us once upon a time! Ye dinna get tae talk tae me like 'at, as ma employer ur no!

NEISH Quite right!

ELIZA Aye, but what did ye dae?

BENYON What was she supposed to do?

ANNIE What was I supposed tae dae?

ELIZA I'd ha nae put up wi 'at!

ANNIE CRUICKSHANK Aye, ye would. Things have mebbe changed in the world…after aw these years…but some things havenae changed at aw.

(The passengers cheerfully form a horse drawn carriage from the past as **ANNIE** *looks around her cheerfully, young, in the moment. The other clearly enjoy this part of her story.)*

I was riding on tap ae the carriage wi ma bag and the coachman. There was a smir of rain aboot in the air, just a suspeecion ae moisture. Pleesant oan ma face. I was excited! The big hoose. I'd been up there before wi ma faither…makin deliveries…and I thought it was wonderful how well dressed and well fed the servants luiked, wi their livery and nice mainners.

I was twelve, neist tae the youngest ae nine ae us. I had twa elder sisters awriddy in service, but I was tae be the special wan. I was tae be ta'en tae the big hoose. My Faither was paid twenty pound for me. At least, that's ma understonnin. I gaithered it fae owre hearin them talk in the carriage.

Folk think because ye dinna spik…ye dinna hear. Oh, ye hear aw right.

(Lighting change as the coach reaches journey's end and we move into the big house below stairs.)

They were aw kind to me that first day. The cook gied me boilings frae a bowl she kept oan the dresser. She stood on a wooden step tae reach thum. Ma faither had gone afore I missed him. But they kept me busy till night time when I cried a wee bit. Naebiddy was surprised tae hear me. They were used tae new lassies crying a wee bit at first. So lang as they didnae mope or get sickly, nae biddy minded.

I'd heard them say there was a lassie. The young mistress. A lassie my age or near it…who couldnae walk. I was quite excited aboot meetin her. But she was a lady as well ae a lassie. I kennt that anaw, young as I wis..

I still wanted tae meet the lassie.

(Servants move around…country house ambience. **ANNIE CRUICKSHANK***, bag in hand, as a wee girl, looks at it.)*

I waited in the kitchen while they talked aboot me. The cook and the footman. Where I was tae stey and such. I was tae be tried oot as a tweeny, a maid ablaw stairs, a servant tae the servants. Cleanin, scourin grates, daein floors and bedding.

And if they found me pleasing, wan day I was tae be taken upstairs tae be introduced tae 'the little mistress.'

They were gie fond ae her. Sorry for her. I gathered that fae their conversations as I worked aroon their feet, as they got used tae me belaw stairs.

Quiet, they said she was. Like me, I thought. She's quiet like me. Maybe I could be her freen.

Her name was Lucy. I fun that oot. I imagined her. Wi that name that sounded sad. I could make her happy. I mind I thought that.

MISTRESS *(Adult.)* My father never liked you.

(no answer.)

Do you hear me?

ANNIE CRUICKSHANK *(Within the scene.)* Aye, mum. I hear you. Yer sayin it every day noo.

MISTRESS 'Something amiss with that girl. Something secretive about her. I don't trust her. I don't like the cut of her jib.'

ANNIE CRUICKSHANK Yes, Mum.

MISTRESS He never liked you. He told me

ANNIE CRUICKSHANK I liked you, Mum. I always did.

MISTRESS Did you? Why did you like me?

ANNIE CRUICKSHANK Not sure why.

MISTRESS Was I ever good to you? Was I ever really good to you?

ANNIE I used tae think so.

*(**ANNIE CRUICKSHANK** weeps.)*

MISTRESS What's bringing this on? Are you crying now?

ANNIE CRUICKSHANK I'm an old woman, Mum.

MISTRESS We're both old women.

(Pause. Deliberately hurtful.)

You're disgusting.

(She checks on the effect her cruelty is having. She is satisfied.)

Go away. Get out.

(Lights out.)

ANNIE CRUICKSHANK *(Resuming her story telling.)* I was near fourteen when I met her for the first time. She was twelve. Sickly. Frae something in her blood. Everyone expected her tae die.

*(**ANNIE CRUICKSHANK** works around the **MISTRESS**. She alternates between telling the story to her fellow passengers, and directly addressing her mistress…or her memory of her.)*

At first…I washed her…soaped her in her bed. Cleaned her white skin. She couldnae…control hersel. She needed me. She needed me like no one has ever needed me. And she seemed tae like me for some reason. She seemed tae want tae please me by getting better.

And ye did. Ye started eating and not wetting yer bed ony merr at night. Ye got better cos of me. Ye owed me yer life. And ye kenned it. Ye loved me. I ken ye did.

Her parents had been waiting for her tae die…like everyone else… They werenae fer comin near her till she was deed ur she'd got better. Thanks tae me, she got better.

Ye were that happy tae see them, and that keen tae show them how well and strong ye were becoming…and how much ye wanted me tae stay wi ye…

They commended me. They bought me a dress. And they got her a tutor…I was in training now, wi her mother's maids. I was to be her maid now…not her nurse

The companion of your bedchamber.

*(**ANNIE CRUICKSHANK** helps **MISTRESS** up.)*

There was a lot tae learn. Fer baith ae us. Talkin right. Lookin right. It wasnae easy. But I loved it. And so did you.

When she was eighteen…I was twenty…it was me that prepared her for your debut. Me who looked at the pictures in the magazines she'd sent for…

And I fun a shape fur yer hair…and I practised on a head I made frae a turnip and some straw…

MISTRESS I don't remember any of that.

ANNIE CRUICKSHANK Ye dee, of course ye dee! Ye were that beautiful. I was that proud!

MISTRESS Were you?

ANNIE CRUICKSHANK Aye…of course…you were aa the world tae me!

MISTRESS You ridiculous woman. What did it have to do with you? Who did you think you were? Who do you think you are now? Hateful, hateful old woman!

(ANNIE narrates alone.)

ANNIE CRUICKSHANK Efter her first dances…receptions… dinners…I came tae her in the mornings wanting tae hear aw aboot it…and she was excited tae tell me everything. The men she'd met… the ither lassies. Tae stert wi onywey. But uch, there was mebbe something aboot her…despite the dowery she brought wi her… the men she met just didnae want tae marry her. Ur mebbe she just didnae find a man she really wanted. No matter how much she wanted tae.

She mebbe wanted it owre much. I don't know.

(ANNIE helps the MISTRESS into a wheelchair.)

Then…right enough… the paralysis…the sickness began coming back tae claim ye.

MISTRESS I was thirty, then…

ANNIE …and I was thirty-two…and we stopped marking your birthday…and we began counting the days…

(ANNIE together with MISTRESS.)

…watching them passing

MISTRESS *(Continuing alone.)* …the sun crossing the sky…

ANNIE Then yer faither bought ye that place in the East Neuk.

MISTRESS 'Spinster Outlook' he called it…

ANNIE And we went tae live there, the two ae us and a wee staff. I was in charge. I did everything for ye. Ye might even say we were happy there. Me taking ye out in yer wheelchair…seein a wee bit ae the world thegither…breathing the sea air.

(ANNIE puts her MISTRESS back to bed. The MISTRESS sleeps. ANNIE strokes her hair.)

A lonely woman…with money…is like fish bait tae some folk. But you had me. You had me tae protect ye. Her parents…forgot ye again.

(She gets up and tidies.)

And it was me they came tae…the thieves…ma ain family, even, that had sold and forgotten me when I was a bairn…Come on, Annie Cruickshank…they said. You've got influence…you've got that auld cripple wrapped aroon yer finger. She'll nivver miss it, quine. She'll never know…But there was naebiddy that mattered tae me the wey that you did.

*(**MISTRESS** wakes.)*

So I don't understand. What did I dee? What changed? Aye…we're getting older the pair ae us… We're old noo. Wir baith old. And age is makin ae us what it does. But I cannae help that. What have I done tae ye that ye treat me so?

MISTRESS I'm sorry.

(Trying to explain.)

But you remind me, every time I see you…that you are all I have. You are not my family. You are not my friend. But you are all I have.

ANNIE CRUICKSHANK I lived my life through you like a mother lives through a child.

MISTRESS But that's not who you are.

ANNIE CRUICKSHANK Who am I, then?

MISTRESS If I were to say I love you, to tell you that I have always loved you…you mean more to me than…anyone…then I would have to confess that all my weary, stony life…has been a lie. I can't do that.

ANNIE CRUICKSHANK *(Angry.)* I could have stole fae you! A hunert times! You would have never even kennt it! I never did. I've never even used your name to get a favour.

MISTRESS Perhaps you should have, perhaps you shouldn't have been so honest.

ANNIE CRUICKSHANK Aren't I your freen? Aren't I the only one who was always here?

MISTRESS *(Angry, clutching at her chest, in pain.)* You're nothing to me. Nothing. I should be nothing to you. Like a cat when its mistress finally dies…Do you know what you should do?

> *(Nastily.)*

You should tear at my flesh when you find me dead. You should eat my eyes.

> *(The **MISTRESS**'s pain becomes overwhelming. She rises up attacking **ANNIE**, then clutching at her chest…she falls back…she is suffering a heart attack. She falls back, yelling at the pain. **ANNIE** holds her as she struggles. The **MISTRESS** throws her off.)*

Let me go!

> *(Suddenly she gasps…and falls back again. But this time she doesn't move. **ANNIE** stares at her **MISTRESS**. Then closes her mouth and eyes. She looks at her again. Then **ANNIE** fetches a carpet bag…and steals silverware, hiding it about her person. She puts on her travelling cloaks and boards the train, with the stage picture – perhaps – returning to the start of the journey. The train ambience and sound returns.)*

ANNIE CRUICKSHANK So here I am. On a train to God Kens where. The first train that came intae the station. Talkin tae masel just like yer faither said I did. Not knowing what tae think. Holding a bag full ae the silverware that I polished every month…and that you never even touched.

For the first time in sixty years…I don't know what I'm doin.

> *(Around her the train dissolves into another transition, but this time to a dance tune, **BENYON** waltzing with the **ELIZA** actress. Then, to the unease of the other passengers, the sinister **MR BENYON** tells a story that they would rather not have to hear. He provokes them by telling it. He begins by recounting his half of a post coital conversation with a woman he met another night.)*

BENYON'S STORY

BENYON Are you crying now?

Yes, you are. I can hear you in the dark.

There's no need to cry, is there? Truly, what do you know now that you didn't know an hour ago?

I did. I knew your wickedness the moment we spoke. Now you now it too. We're all the same. Wickedness calls to wickedness.

The first? No, love. You're not the first. And you'll not be the last.

*(There is a scream from **ELIZA** that mixes with the shriek of train whistle. Lights snap up to the train state. Train sounds and music. **BENYON** addresses his captive audience.)*

I keep thinking that somebody's going to stop me. But nobody does. Nobody ever sees me for what I am.

Why can't you tell? Doesn't it show in a distortion of the features? Wickedness like mine? Doesn't it radiate from every pore?

In the army it was the same. In India all anyone could see was my round, innocent face. Even the soldiers…the mutineers. Even as we chained them on the front of the cannons. Even moments before we blew them to hell, they smiled at me. They thought that somebody who looked as nice as I did…was going to save them.

I learned in India that this…surface of things…

(He pinches his skin.)

…is all anyone sees of anything. Beneath the skin, their skin, they hated us…they had always hated us underneath the smiles and skin…that's why they rose against us…and when we punished them for it, we turned them inside out…

And now, twenty years later, everywhere I go in these rainy islands, I still discover things I don't even want to see. But they show themselves to me. Everywhere. Even in Wales.

The length and width of England, Scotland and Ireland I've travelled, my samples in my suitcase. My bad memories waking me up at night. And everywhere I go, I think here, finally, in these grey streets of this grey town, amid this fog of another night...somebody will stop me.

But here I am. On the narrow road to the North once again. What was her name, the one in Aberdeen? I really should remember. I really should remember them all.

Where might she and I meet? The next one? At some social occasion, perhaps? At dinner. In some hotel dining room at breakfast. Or in some low tavern where as our eyes seek each other out. As heat seeks heat.

Why not on this train? That woman there. This one. That one. It hardly matters.

It would be so much...nicer...not to know...that lust walks among us...When a silver spoon drops into the jam pot...when we help one another to tea...pulses quickening unconfessed, eyes flickering, cheeks flushing...it would be so much more...tasteful.

But nature makes demands. Nature will be satisfied. It astonishes me. That you still pretend that the world is other than it is. That you are surprised...flattered, even, by my attention...as if such contact were new to you, as if our animal nature...were a revelation.

As if you didn't know...I hate you so. All of you.

That woman in Southampton...so wide eyed...so impressed...yes... impressed with me for revealing her own nature to her. Revealing what she was. Turning her inside out.

Somebody should stop me. You should stop me. I should stop myself.

(He speaks with the rhythm of the train wheels.)

Which one shall it be? Which one shall it be? Which one shall it be?

(The train sound continues. We leave **BENYON** *to his thoughts.* **ELIZA** *looks at* **EMILY***, trying to read her from her appearance, reflecting on herself.)*

ELIZA Look at her. She's that beautiful. And when she smiles tae hersel at some thought she's hivin...that smile lights up the train.

I bet she'd no wait. No for any man tae make up his mind. No for nothin. I bet she'd no wait for whatever was gien her and say thank you for it.

Naebiddy ever accused me ae bein beautiful. They used tae laugh at me, walk behind me at school makkin fun ae how I walked. Cuz wan ae ma leg's a bit short cos it was broke when I wiz a bairn.

Nae biddy ivver made fun ae her. Look at her. That's what I'd like tae be. When I'm her age.

I was lucky mebbe, that I wasnae pretty. Ur the boys would have been efter me like they were the other girls…till they fell pregnant… and showin thersels suitable ae bearing the bairns a fermer needs tae work his fields, they got mairrit.

That wasnae fer me. I was lucky. What was fer me was this. Service.

Service, they cry it…What am I? A slave. Tae ma faither I was a slave tae be used and then sold, and noo I'm workin fer somebody else's family daein aw the things I used to dae fer mine…and fer whit? Fer a chance tae dae the same forever? In somebody else's hoose? Wi somebody else's bairns?

I'm no daein it forever. I'm no. There has to be another way. There has tae be.

(She looks at **EMILY***.)*

What's her secret? God! What does she know that I don't know?

EMILY'S STORY for ELIZA

EMILY *(Answering her.)* God will find a way to punish me. One day. I know He will.

(She smiles.)

But so far…nothing. Not a hint of the Lord's displeasure has fallen on my head. One might almost think that He wasn't paying attention.

(Directly to **ELIZA***.)*

Are *you* paying attention?

(She begins her performance, cueing music. The passengers are participants in that performance. But the audience is **ELIZA**, **EMILY**'s *focus reverting to her periodically.)*

The four and twentieth day of May, of all days of the year, sir,

A virgin lady, fresh and gay, did privately appear, sir.

(Spoken.)

(The **CAST** *whisper his sinister name.)*

Mr Abercrombie is a liar and a thief. He is dangerous. He is ruthless and ambitious and emphatically not to be trusted. There had to be some reason for us to rub along so well.

(She sings, now with minimal accompaniment.)

Hard by a riverside got she, and did sing loud, the rather,

For she was sure she was secure, and had intent to bath her.

(Spoken.)

You heard his name in whispers…Abercrombie!

(The **CAST**, *encouraged by* **EMILY**, *echo the sinister name of 'Abercrombie' in whispers.)*

When one heard of a sudden death…or an eviction by night where the tenants simply… vanished…one sensed Abercrombie's hand… swift, sudden, sure… 'That will be Abercrombie's work! That smells of Abercrombie!'

CAST *(Whisper to each other.)* Abercrombie!

EMILY Mother and Father disappeared when we were still small children, my sisters and myself…and we were taken from the lap of comparative luxury in rented rooms at the top of one of those tall houses on the High Street, to a baby farm at the very bottom of the Cowgate. I don't know the truth of what happened. If Mr Abercrombie was involved! I have a memory of a bright room, and of a dark corridor. Of screaming, and terror. Of being lost in the dark…I was very young then.

(Sings, the music fuller.)

With glittering glancing jealous eyes, she shyly looks about, sir,

To see if any lurking spies were hid to find her out, sir.

(Spoken.)

What I do remember ...from being not that much older...is work. Work first in a laundry deep below the street, my fingers raw and swollen. Tubbing. Dying. I remember being beaten and being told to be thankful to God for each blow. Then being farmed out to good Christian folk running a good Christian enterprise...aged eight running between the looms of a mill, picking out oose from shuttles and frames whose sharp edges came so very close to severing my fingers...and running away from there. I remember running... through dark and silent streets expecting murder at every turn and wynd...attracted by the distant sounds of laughter...music...

(Sings, with increasingly lush musical backing.)

And being well resolved that none could see her nakedness, sir,

She pulled her robes off, one by one, and did herself undress, sir.

(Spoken.)

I attached myself to women of the night, women whose morality fell far below that of the mill workers, but who rarely had their limbs severed in the course of their labour. I made myself useful to these women. I fetched and carried and cleaned for them...I carried water, I went to markets, I stole and acted as their agent in legitimate and illegitimate purchases. I made myself necessary to the brightest butterflies I could find. 'These are the favourites' I said to myself... 'These are the ones I must emulate. These are the ones who will one day rise above the herd and catch themselves a gentleman.'

(Sings.)

Into the fluent stream she leapt, she looked like Venus' glass, sir.

The fishes from all quarters crept to see so fair a lass, sir.

(Spoken.)

Then one of them did just that! Rosalie...who spoke a little French and had picked up a trick or two...and kept herself clean...Very importantly...snared a gentleman. And I went with her to a set of rooms in Stockbridge...as her hairdresser and dress maker. And I learned everything I could from her.

(Sings.)

Each fish did wish himself a man, about her all were drawn, sir.

And at the sight of her began to spread about their spawn, sir.

Aged around fourteen, I fell victim to the affections of Mistress Rosalie's master. I don't know if she was complicit in the transaction...but I found myself...once he had tasted of me... shared...as a nubile novelty...passed around his friends...like a plate of sandwiches at cards. While Rosalie...whom I had allowed myself to love...watched. With drugged eyes and a sad smile.

(Cold, angry.)

Aged fifteen, I found myself delivered of a child. I was no longer marketable as a nymphet. I cannot even guess the father's identity. I never saw who she resembled. They took her from me. I scarcely saw her for ten minutes, ten minutes when I fed her from the breast...just once...to be raised, no doubt, to the same estate as her poor mother.

I sometimes catch myself...I do sometimes wonder where she might be. If she is happy. Safe. Alive, even.

Then, for a time, I became a common prostitute.

One doesn't like to think about it. One keeps such memories... compartmentalised...so that one's griefs do not interfere with the business of the day...But sometimes, despite oneself...

(Sings, now with full accompaniment.)

A lad that long her love had been and could obtain no grace, sir,

For all her prying lay unseen, hid in a secret place, sir.

Who had often been repulsed when he had come to woo her,

Pulled off his clothes and furiously did run and leap into her.

She squeaked, she cried, and down she dived, he brought her up again, sir.

He brought her up upon the shore, and then, and then, and then, sir.

As Adam did old Eve enjoy, you may guess what I mean, sir;

Because she all uncovered lay, he covered her again, sir.

(Spoken.)

That's the trouble with trains. They are, no doubt, a modern miracle of engineering…but…they take time…and during the journey… one starts thinking about all manner of things. All kinds of secret boxes open…

(She drifts into a memory. Shivers at it. Recovers. Smiles.)

Anyway, after a time…I taught myself to speak and to sing. To be an actress…I found my way to the stage. And, at last, to Mr Abercrombie.

It was Mr Abercrombie who arranged that his Lordship attend one of my performances in his exclusive little cabaret. He knew his man. He knew that I would be to his master's taste. He thereby secured his position as his Lordship's factor…and respectability came in my reach! From Rosalie to the theatre to his Lordship…his kept woman, his favoured mistress. His Lordship installed me in rooms on the High Street that I fancied were the very rooms my sisters and I had occupied as children. I was a recovered phoenix, so long as my feathers were bright…

(Sings, a cappella once more.)

With watered eyes, she pants and cries, 'I'm utterly undone, sir,

If you will not be wed to me by the next morning sun, sir.'

He answered her, he would not stir out of her sight till then, sir.

'We'll both clasp hands in wedlock bands, marry, and to it again, sir.'

EMILY *returns to her seat.*

And now, Mr Abercrombie has taken one last chattel from his lordship's portfolio. Me. Now he has…me…

It had always been His Lordship's intention to deliver me unto his servant once he was done with me. And I give myself credit that it has taken twenty years and not five…or ten…for Mr Abercrombie to take possession. He has offered me…marriage. Success, as the world measures it. We are to be married in Kirriemuir on Saturday next.

(To **ELIZA***.)*

You look at me with wondering eyes. And, yes! I have survived. I never expected to survive. But consequently, I have grown older.

And I dread being old. I dread it so. To be old and poor and alone in this world is not to be thought of.

At one end of the line is my old life…and waiting for me at the station in Dundee… is another. In between these lives…is the train. The dark and noisy hiatus of the train.

I always thought that God would find a way to punish me. Now perhaps he has.

GEORGE AND ELIZA'S STORY

Transition We see **ELIZA***'s fate in the disaster, then her return to a happy memory of a tryst with her beau,* **GEORGE***. They kiss. They nestle together.*

GEORGE What are ye thinkin'?

ELIZA You're daft

GEORGE I'm ur? I'm daft?

ELIZA Yer no right. Yer mither must've drapped ye oan yer heid.

GEORGE Ah'm daft?

ELIZA Oh uhhuh!

GEORGE You're the wan that's daft.

ELIZA If I am, it's your fault.

GEORGE How dae ye mekk that oot?

ELIZA I wasnae daft afore I met you.

GEORGE I dinna ken that. I've nae but your word for that.

ELIZA Ask anybody.

GEORGE I will.

ELIZA It's catchin. Daftness.

GEORGE Is it?

ELIZA Ma hale life is ruint…ye've ruined me wi daftness.

GEORGE Have I?

ELIZA Oh aye.

GEORGE How dae I ken that?

ELIZA Whit dae ye mean?

GEORGE How dae ah ken ye werenae daft already? Ye were daft the minute we met.

ELIZA The minute we met…there! Ye've proved it.

GEORGE I've proved nothing.

ELIZA There ye are…

GEORGE Aa'l I ken is, the moment I met ye, ye wer daft

ELIZA And you love me furrit.

GEORGE What does that prove? Except I'm daft…

*(Lights fade on the lovers. Train ambience. **ELIZA** reads. As she does, her book comes to life, selling her a new and better life.)*

AMERICAN SALESMAN (NEISH.)/ELIZA *reading*: Nature has done for California all that could be asked at her hands. Suitable immigrants who make the journey here are assured of a hearty handshake and a warm welcome. We need immigrants of kindred races who will locate themselves and their families permanently upon the soil.

*(In real time, on the train, **BENYON** approaches her.)*

BENYON It's a nasty night out there, isn't it?

*(**ELIZA** tries to ignore him.)*

Are you cold? Come now, it's a simple question

ELIZA I'm quite comfortable. Thank you, sir.

BENYON Are you sure you're warm enough?

ELIZA Yes, thank you…

BENYON I have a blanket.

ELIZA Oh, aye? Hiv ye?

BENYON Big enough for both of us.

ELIZA No, thank you.

BENYON And for added warmth, I have a little drop of cognac. Do you know the taste of cognac?

ELIZA Mister. Where d'ye think this patter is gonnae get ye?

BENYON What I might offer you later is up to you.

(She turns away from him.)

ELIZA I'm meeting my fiancé.

BENYON Are you, now?

ELIZA He's gettin on the train at the next stop.

BENYON Who is the lucky chap? Why has he left you all alone?

ELIZA He's been visitin his mither.

*(**BENYON** sits beside her.)*

Who tellt ye ye could sit doon?

BENYON You did.

ELIZA I don't think so!

BENYON You did, you know. Or you never told me not to. Is he very good to you?

ELIZA Of course!

BENYON But is he as nice as me? Will an evening spent with him end as nicely as an evening spent with me?

(Pause.)

Did you quarrel with him when last you spoke?

ELIZA *(Taken aback.)* Naw.

BENYON You did, didn't you?

ELIZA *(Recovering.)* Folk are lookin!

BENYON You could do so much better than some argumentative rustic.

ELIZA George is a mechanic!

BENYON Is he, now?

ELIZA Yes.

BENYON I'm a salesman.

ELIZA Ye don't say?

BENYON Have you been making plans, the two of you?

ELIZA Wir going to America.

BENYON Heavens! Are you travelling tonight?

(She turns away and reads. The **AMERICAN SALESMAN** *pipes up.)*

SALESMAN The present population of California is sparse; and there is the more room therefore for the growth of trade, and more opportunities for new comers to establish themselves in business.

(Her beau **GEORGE** *appears. He and* **BENYON** *are like her good and bad angels.)*

GEORGE Ach, no! Is that book whit I think it is?

ELIZA They'll pey for the passage, it says. Aw roon the cape tae California.

GEORGE For God's sake, Eliza! What d'y wanni spile oor day oot fer?

ELIZA I'm no spiling onythin.

(He gets up. She stands with him. He is angry the good news he has for her is being spoiled.)

George…What is it?

(He hesitates. He didn't want it to be like this. But he's stuck now, so….)

GEORGE I've been offered a start at Camperdown. There. See? I kenned that would dumstooner ye!

ELIZA Camperdown?

GEORGE Cox Brothers ae Camperdown. Aye. In Lochee. Not in America!

ELIZA Daein what?

GEORGE In the shop. Assistant engineer.

ELIZA Assistant?

GEORGE Weel…assistant tae the assistant engineer…

ELIZA In the mill?

GEORGE Course in the mill! Maintenance. Repair.

ELIZA I see.

GEORGE It's a good job…

ELIZA I'm no stupit. I ken it's a good job.

GEORGE There's hunerts walkin aboot unemployed, Eliza.

ELIZA You're not unemployed.

GEORGE I'm no the noo…

ELIZA George…

GEORGE Eliza! Can ye no accept guid news when ye hear it. It's the biggest, safest employer in the city. They'll be there forever!

ELIZA But ye know…It's not what I want.

GEORGE This is better. D'ye hear me? It's in yer hon! It's no…pie in the sky…Christ! I kennt ye'd be like this! I kennt ye'd…Ye should be dancing. Ye should be happy for us! I should be happy! I deserve tae be happy. For me! For you! We can be mairit noo. Finally. And look at at ye. Look at us! Wir fightin aboot it.

ELIZA It isnae enough.

GEORGE God's sake! Enough fer what. It's the best job a man could hope tae get!

ELIZA In Lochee.

GEORGE Lochee is where we live! Why don't ye want tae be happy?

(We return to real time on the train.)

BENYON You're restless, aren't you? I can tell that by looking at you. I'm restless too. I'm never satisfied.

ELIZA Look, Mister…

BENYON Benyon. Benyon is my name. I'm very persistent. If I meet someone I like.

ELIZA You're just bored. That's aw. Yer bored and yer rich and yer a bit fou.' Yer not really interested in me.

BENYON You have no idea what I'm interested in.

ELIZA And ye think gien me a hard time will pass the time the night fer ye. Cos ye think I'm a daft wee lassie ye can tease. Well. I'm no playin.

BENYON Dinner, then. What about a spot of dinner? In that big, new hotel near the station. The Queen's Hotel. A nice hot bath. A big, clean bed with cool, clean sheets…That's how I'm planning the rest of my evening after this tiresome journey.

ELIZA I'm not interested.

BENYON Oh yes, you are. You're tempted. Aren't you? You're thinking about it.

*(He laughs. **ELIZA** turns to **GEORGE**, standing angrily. Lighting change.)*

ELIZA Mechanics have their ain hooses in California, George! Are you gonnae get that in Lochee? Will your assisting the assistant engineer in Camperdown get you and me a hoose? Or will it just rent a room for you…while I stay cooped up in the attic ae somebody else's hoose.

GEORGE In time…

ELIZA We dinna hiv time!

GEORGE What? Yer not expectin, are ye…?

ELIZA Whit if I was? What if there was a bloody baby coming? Whit wad ye dae?

(He stares at her. Eventually.)

No…I'm not expectin'.

GEORGE What dae ye mean, then, 'we don't have time'?

ELIZA Time gets wore away. No' just wi bairns. Time gets eaten.

GEORGE What are ye on aboot?

ELIZA Wan day in twenty years …if ye havnae cut yer erm aff fixin a carder, ye'll still be a mechanic at Camperdown. And ye'll still be somebody else's man. Ye'll still be Cox's man!

GEORGE Twenty years work isna naethin. You ask onybiddy.

ELIZA I dinna want you tae be anybody's man but mine.

GEORGE Ye cannae think like that. The warld's no like that.

ELIZA I dae think like that. I'll no have slavery for me, and I'll no have it fer you.

GEORGE They pay guid wages...

ELIZA They own ye. Yer life is not yer ain.

GEORGE Eliza...

ELIZA Whit?

GEORGE What else is there?

> (**ELIZA** *turns between the siren voices of the* **SALESMAN**, **BENYON** *and* **GEORGE**.)

AMERICAN SALESMAN We invite all who desire information concerning the resources of California to apply to us or our agents, by letter or in person, and we shall take pleasure in assisting them.

BENYON I can read you like you can read that book...you dream of somewhere warm, bright...where you can be free. Don't you... Where you can be naked.

ELIZA Aw, fuck off!

BENYON Where you can be yourself, then! Where you can be as honest and brave as you really are. No more bowing and scraping to your betters. No more pretending you believe in ministers and churches...in empires and upstairs and downstairs...a place where you can believe in yourself...

I'm offering you that...for tonight...for one night only...in the best hotel in the city...What you decide to do tomorrow...is tomorrow's. Sufficient unto the day is the pleasure thereof...

ELIZA *(To* **GEORGE**.*)* You are askin me tae settle fer spendin the rest ae ma life thinkin what might hae been.

GEORGE Aye...well mebbe ye should find yerself some adventurer... wha'll travel the world wi ye and never...

ELIZA Never what?

GEORGE Be steady.

ELIZA Steady? Like you? Like ma faither? Is that what ye mean? My faither pulled a cart a hundred hours a week. The high point of oor steady week was a Sabbath visit tae the cemetery tae celebrate the steady dead.

BENYON I am not offering to use you, my dear...I am offering that tonight you use me to get what you want...Don't tell me that doesn't intrigue you...just a little...

GEORGE That's...

ELIZA That's whit? That's just me? That's you anaw...You wi yer faither fermin every hour, burying yer brothers and sisters...

BENYON Give yourself up to your nature. To who you really are... Wouldn't it be liberating...not to be hungry...just for a night...

ELIZA Once ye've been at Camperdown a year, ye'll get used tae it... ye'll think the wages could be worse, ye'll think the wee room ye can rent isnae that bad ...and ye'll see me on ma days aff...but in ten years time, whit'll ye be daein? Ye'll be daein the same work for the same money in the same place drinkin the same wages. Well ye'll no be daein it wi me waitin oan ye. Or waiting on anybody. I'll no be here.

GEORGE Where will ye be? Who'll ye be wi?

ELIZA I mebbe hivnae met them yet.

GEORGE Are you finishin wi me, Eliza? Are you honest tae God feenishin wi me...because I've fun a job?

ELIZA Doors slam somewhere else in the hoose when ye open the front door.

GEORGE I havenae said yes tae Cox's yet. I said I'd speak tae...

ELIZA Tae me?

GEORGE Tae my mither.

ELIZA The future willna wait oan you talkin tae your mither, George. It disnae dae that. If ye hesitate, it comes for ye just the same.

GEORGE What dae you want from me, Eliza?

ELIZA I'm visiting my family in Kingsbarn on Sunday coming. You go and see yer mither in Wormit. You meet me on the train at St Fort at the back o seven. And you tell me then what you want. And then we'll baith ken.

(GEORGE leaves her…disappearing from her memory. Now the only reality is the train in the present tense. She turns to BENYON. He stands.)

BENYON When we get to Dundee, I'll get off the train first…and I'll meet you outside the station. And then I can promise you an experience like nothing you have ever known.

(He makes to go.)

ELIZA Mister…? What if I said yes…what if I said I wanted my freedom…I wanted tae be me forever and ever and ever. What wad ye say then…Mister Salesman?

BENYON Forever is a long time. Any man who promises you anything past tomorrow morning…is a liar.

*(The train comes to a sudden, screeching halt. Everyone is thrown forward. **EMILY** is thrown into **NEISH**. **BENYON** onto **ELIZA**. They laugh and recover. The lines enclosed by brackets in bold are spoken simultaneously.)*

ELIZA *(To BENYON, **still holding her**.)* **Let go ae me, please… yer no gonnae faa doon!**

*(BENYON **lets her go**.)*

EMILY *(To NEISH.)* **That was sudden!**

NEISH Perhaps the driver was late seeing the signal.)

(ANNIE CRUIKSHANK It's a dirty night out there, right enough!

BENYON What are stopping here for?.)

NEISH This is St Fort.

(GEORGE boards the train, looking for ELIZA.)

They'll be by tae collect tickets before we cross the bridge…

GEORGE Eliza!

ELIZA *goes to him firmly.*

ELIZA George Johnstone! I am telling you now, you are going to need tae tell me now what you want tae do or you and me are finished!

GEORGE Yes.

ELIZA *(Still angry.)* Yes, whit?

GEORGE *(Angry too.)*

Name ae God! I'll marry ye and we'll go tae America. Right?

(She hesitates.)

I'm sayin 'yes' tae ye, Eliza... I dinna care a damn whit Cox Brothers or ma mither think. God help us.

*(**ELIZA** hugs him.)*

ELIZA Oh, He WILL, George. He will.

GEORGE He'd fuckin better!

*(**ELIZA** sees that everyone is looking at herself and **GEORGE**.)*

ELIZA *(Announces to the carriage.)* Everybody... Sorry. This young man and I are just now engaged tae be married.

(General congratulations. Passengers stand.)

EMILY *(Who is nearest, kissing her.)* Congratulations.

> **BENYON** *moves past her to kiss* **ELIZA**. *And as she watches him, and* **GEORGE** *and* **ELIZA**, *she makes the decision she's been thinking of.*

BENYON May I add my congratulations to the both of you...

EMILY *(To **NEISH**.)* Could you...Young man...would you mind helping me off with my bag?

NEISH Surely.

> *As* **NEISH** *gets her bag,* **GEORGE** *and* **ELIZA** *embrace and* **ANNIE, MRS EASTON** *and* **BENYON** *applaud.*

EMILY Do you know if there is a service back to Edinburgh tonight?

NEISH *(As he lifts her bag down.)* I think so. Let me put this on the platform for ye.

EMILY You're very kind. I'm sorry for your loss, whatever it was.

> *(**EMILY** makes to follow* **NEISH** *and to leave the train,* **ELIZA** *intercepts her, holds her arm.)*

ELIZA Good luck. Whatever it is yer goin'.

> **EMILY** *smiles and leaves the train.* **NEISH** *returns to his seat.*

BENYON Can I ask if everyone will take a drink with me? Come, now! It's a cold night…

    *(To **ELIZA**.)*

Will you at least take a drink with me, my dear? Will you console me that much?

    *(To the carriage as the train leaves the station. We see **EMILY** on the platform watching them go. She turns and leaves the stage with her bag.)*

Will all of you take a drink…to what might have been! And to what instead will be.

ANNIE CRUIKSHANK *(Produces silver cups from her bag.)* Here…I've got cups…

ELIZA These are nice!

    *(**BENYON** pours and sings.)*

BENYON Ye coopers and hoopers, attend to my ditty,
    I sing o'a cooper wha dwelt in Dundee;
    This young man he was baith am'rous and witty,
    He pleased the fair maids wi the blink o' his e'e.

    *(**GEORGE** and **ELIZA** join in with the next verse. **MRS EASTON** listens, lifted by their celebratory mood.)*

BENYON, GEORGE, ELIZA
    He was nae but a cooper, a common tub-hooper,
    The most o'his trade lay in pleasin' the fair;
    He hoopt them, he coopt them, he bort them, he plugt them,
    They' a' sent for Sandy when out o'repair.

    *(They cajole **ANNIE** into joining their singing the next verse.)*

    For a twelvemonth or sae this youth was respected,
    An' he was as busy, as weel he could be;
    But bus'ness increased so that some were neglected,
    Which ruined his trade in the town o'Dundee.

    The music continues. Theme music is mixed in with the music hall tune.

NEISH That's us on the bridge. We're on the bridge now!

    (Music. The song continues mixed with the theme.)

COMPANY A baillie's fair daughter she wanted a coopin',

And Sandy was sent for, as oft time was he;
He yerkt her sae hard that she sprung an end-hoopin'
Which banish'd poor Sandy frae bonnie Dundee.

*(They laugh. The wind rises, drowning them out. Then there is a
screaming of metal. We have a last image of terrible realization. Mrs Easton's
manuscript is blown away into the wind. BLACKOUT. End Play.)*

The Signalman

The Signalman was first performed on Monday 23 September 2019 at Òran Mór, Glasgow as part of A Play, A Pie and a Pint. It transferred to the Traverse Theatre, Edinburgh on Tuesday 1 October.

Cast	Tom McGovern
Director	Ken Alexander

Scotland 1919. **THOMAS BARCLAY**, *a signalman with the North British Railway, is in his signal cabin on the South side of the Tay Bridge lying on his cot listening to the wind outside. The bell sounds twice. He sits up and goes to respond. He rings his own bell. He sits back down.*

THOMAS Forty year ago? Forty year ago tonight? I cannae even mind who I was. Sixty-four now…sixty-four. Cannae believe that either! Spry as paint, mind. Walkin, cyclin' every day…gaun back tae penny farthin days…up and doon the river front. I'm no done yet. I've years ahead ae me yet! Unless something happens. Accidents… happen…

Forty year ago. Who can even mind ae sic a thing? I wasnae even marrit yet! Hadnae had a son…and twa daughters…that lived onyway…or grandbairnies…the auldest yin grown tae manhood… and noo…it's noo I'm mindin ae it. Fer some reason. Forty year ago. Forty year ago tonight.

Mebbe that's it. Mebbe that's aw it is. The anniversary. December 28th…1879… 'which will be remembered for a very long time.'

Aye, for a bloody criminal offense against the craft ae poetry if naethin else…

But forty year I've sat here winter nights in this cabin…tending tae ma signals…changing the points doon there…heavier than they once were, right enough…listenin fer the bell…

The bell…

Listenin tae the wind. Hell ae a blouster some nichts. Hell ae a thing.

(He shivers, uncomfortable.)

Why is it? Why is ma skin crawlin?

What's the time?

Jesus, I'm sweatin. What's up wi me? Did I owre stoke the fire?

(He looks around.)

It's no chinged, of course. Ma cabin…ma signal box…it's just the same. It's oan the same wee jink ae track…the same wee headland juttin oot…intae the Firth…the single track…ootbye…ontae the new brig…ten or so foot tae the richt ae the auld yin…that's aa…it looks the same. Looks the same oot ae ma windae.

Christ, get a hold ae yeself, min! Goat the heeby jeebies for some reason!

Course…no aabiddy has a permanent record of theirsels at twenty-four year auld the likes o I dee. A permanent record. Ma words, as I spoke them…as a loon ae twenty-four…scared oot ma wits…no just by whit I'd seen as much as aw they people listening tae me…aw they lawyers and judges in their wigs and goons.

And aw ae them angry…they were aw angry…that was it…I mind it noo…they were aw angry. I didnae ken what they were angry aboot. I didnae ken if they were angry wi me! Had I done something wrang? I didnae ken! Only God really kens yon kinna hing! But lawyers and judges mek oot they bloody dee.

Mebbe I hud! Aw these clever men, wi their education and their Latin tags…they were aw angry aboot something…and they were aw lookin at me.

Coorse, I unnerston noo. They were humiliated. Their brig across space, their engineering marvel…their brig intae the future they thocht they hid aa sorted oot…it was aw tangled and broken in the river…and they had tae be angry wi somebody for that… somebody had let them doon! It was like when the Titanic sank…the unsinkable Titanic!

And at that moment, oan that first Monday ae the enquiry…the first Monday ae the New Year ae 1880…Christ, aw that time gone… they were angry wi whoever was fool eneuch tae get papped in front ae them. Ony unfortunate bugger they could get a haud ae. They'd lost their bridge, they'd lost a train…aw they folk…aw they payin passengers…whose relatives micht sue them aw tae buggery… and somebody had to tek the high jump, somebody hid tae be tae blame…

The day afore that, in the kirk…as I think oan it noo…in aw the kirks across Scotland…aw the ministers…established, free and wee…_they_ aw knew who tae blame. Christ aye! It was God! He'd done it! 'Divine Providence.' It was a judgment, ye see, a judgment on aw they folk workin on a Sunday, travellin on a Sunday. It was a judgment. His Mighty Haun had swept doon in the form ae wund fae heaven or Siberia and battered a train full ae sinners intae God's Holy Watter! God had taken the shape ae a storm and punished them aw...punished me. I hud tae sit there and listen tae that!

Jings! Nae bloody wunner I was nervous the neist day! I was nervous taking the ferry wi ma Mither and Faither...in case his mighty hand would dee a repeat performance! Aye...I went wi ma parents! A grown mannie ae twenty-four! But I had the Almighty comin efter me. I needed aw the help I could get!

They called us aw first, ye see...the 'servants ae the company'... the employees ae the North British Railway...weel...they kennt fine how tae get hold ae us...we wernae gaun onywhere. They could find us! We werenae in the south ae France like the architect and shareholders searching fer the winter sun...

So we were first. Station staff...signal staff...even a driver was oan the stand just afore I was...no the driver they wanted, of course, no him, he was at the bottom ae the river...past bein shouted at! Naebiddy's corpse had even come up yet! What they got was the driver ae the train before...the wan crossin the other wey, the wan that had passed my signal box afore six that nicht...gaun the other way ...wi the rain beatin at it...the wind rippin ye aff the grun...and I'd rung the bell tae say he was safe...he was safely across...

What was his name?

(Looks at book.)

It was my folks. They got me this. Wrote away tae His Maijesty's stationers in London fer a copy o the evidence I'd gien. What the hell did they want tae dee that fer? Why the hell did they sit there, the pair ae them, in the enquiry, in the courtroom...tae listen tae me. I mind walking tae tek the stand, I mind keekin up and seein ma Da...aw reed in the face, beamin like an idiot...

Because I was important aw ae a sudden. A mere signalman! I was important. Aa these clever folk in wigs and goons were asking me questions...like I was important...like I was tae blame...and he sat there wi ma Ma beside him in a new bonnet...smiling like an arse, he was...I can see him...reed in the puss like he aye was wi his hairt condition...he wasnae lang fer this warld...and I looked up tae see him...and ma Ma waved at me...she waved! Like I was at the fuckin seaside! She must ae thought she was being supportive, but I felt like bein sick, I could feel it risin up ma thrapple and ah blushed…God, ah blushed! I mind it noo…I blushed like a fuckin wee lassie…

I could feel it! stairtin in ma feet…I could feel it… climbin up ma legs, a big body sized reedy, and it was up ma tummy and ma chist, like a crawlin wave ae fire and then it was oot ma collar and gaun up my neck…turnt ma heid intae a picklt beetroot…and ma face…my eyes, ma cheeks…then it was breakin…explodin oot ma hale heid like a nimbus ae sweat roon an angel…I had tae clutch oan tae the rail.

I was sweatin like I'd just run twenty mile!

I mind a that noo… like it was yisterday. Maybe it was yisterday as God and his angels coont the days…but by Christ, I was just a boy. And they were aw lookin at me.

(He plays the parts of his younger self and of the lawyer questioning him, referring to the book, but stays within character…i.e. Thomas Barclay is playing the lawyer…not the actor playing Thomas Barclay. However, as he does, he is gradually returning to that moment forty years ago.)

What is your name?

My name is Thomas Barclay.

How old are you?

Twenty-four.

You are a signalman employed by the North British Railway Company?

Yes, sir

Where is your station?

Tay Bridge. At the South End.

What have you to do there, as a signalman?

Signalling to the train and on the telegraph. That the line is clear… and safe.

Including the line…onto the bridge…?

Yes, sir.

And over it?

Yes, sir.

You've been at the South cabin since the bridge was opened? Is that right?

Yes, sir.

Some eighteen months?

Yes, sir.

And have you ever observed, in that time…boisterous weather?

(He laughs.)

Aye that's the fuckin word for it. I kennt it was something…but that's what it wis… 'Boisterous!' It's what lawyers dee, o' course. They lead ye through the story…mak ye tell it again, piece by piece…but even as yer tellin it, it sounds… wrang…like yer lyin! Ye feel like a liar. That's not how it was, ye want to say, that's not how it was at all…

(As lawyer.)

Have you ever known the wind to be so boisterous as to oscillate a train from side to side?

No, sir.

You havenae?

I've not seen it, sir.

You've never crossed the bridge by train in a high wind? Or observed such oscillation?

I've not observed such a thing, but I've heard aboot it.

We are not here to hear what you may have heard. We are here for your personal witness.

I fuckin ken that…!

(Correctly, now wholly in the moment.)

Yes, sir. I was on duty…I was at ma work…on the 28th ae December 1879. It was my duty, in particular, to let pass the train that was coming up from Burntisland …at a few minutes past seven, I was in my cabin. The signal from St Fort was at eight minutes past seven. I recorded it.

You noted it?

It was my duty to note it. The signal I received was the one to tell me that the train had aariddy left…and soon would enter that part ae the line…for which I was…

(As lawyer, as his own conscience.)

For which you were responsible?

(Pause. He collects himself. The wind gets louder. And **THOMAS** *begins to relive his movements.)*

Afore I allowed the train tae pass ma cabin, I telegraphed tae the North side of the bridge to check if the line ahead were clear and safe. And received confirmation by the bell…by two chimes of the signal bell.

(The bell sounds twice.)

The train reached my cabin at thirteen minutes past seven. And slowed doon ti receive the train staff to gie it permission to cross the bridge. It passed my cabin at aboot…three or four miles an hour, at the usual pace at which a train passed tae receive permission tae cross…I walked along side…holdin up the train staff…I passed it to the crew as usual…and the train accelerated onto the bridge at, so far as I could tell…the regulation speed of twenty-five miles per hour.

(At the inquiry.)

The train staff?

A small stick… a token…

A baton?

Aye. I had to gie the driver a baton as his warrant for crossin the bridge… The train staff we call it.

Did you give the 'train staff' to the driver?

Tae the stoker. He leaned oot for it. The driver was occupied. I saw the driver. He nodded at me. He may huv smiled. I thought he did smile in the light ae the fire. I knew him.

David Mitchell?

Yes.

Did you know the stoker, George Ness?

No. He seemed verra young. Even younger than me.

(As the lawyer, aggressively.)

Was there anything in the demeanour of the company's servants or in the state of the train to attract your attention? Did you notice the number of carriages? Any particular quality or quantity of the passengers...as the train slowly passed away from you. And accelerated onto the bridge?

(The lighting changes as we return **THOMAS BARCLAY** *to the night of the disaster.)*

I didnae see onythin. I wasnae worried aboot onythin. I didnae pay any special attention...tae who was....how many...I didnae look. I had nae reason...besides...It was a dirty night...

I went back inside. It was my duty was tae send a signal tae the other side. Tae the North side of the bridge. I rang the signal bell. Tae indicate that the train was on its wey.

I also sent a signal back to the station South...tae St Fort, that the line was now clear atween the station and the brig. Each signalman sends first tae the signalman ahead...and then tae the one behind. Then... I went and cleared up the stove in my cabin...and prepared to put on a fresh fire. I had wan merr train tae wait oan that nicht. I raked oot the ashes efter I had marked my book and shut my points. That is, the points to let the train come on.

Then I saw somethin. As I stood up fae tendin the fire...I saw something ...through the windae. Just for a moment. I thought I saw somethin. Oan the bridge. I thought I saw sparks...

Sparks? Did you say sparks...?

Ye couldnae see the brig itsel. It was dark...wi the wind...the rain... but I thought I saw sparks...very bright....sudden...and a moment later...the tail light ae the train...vanished. I thought mebbe that the train had descended...doon the incline towards the North side...The light often disappeared at that point...but it seemed...owre soon...

I didnae like to think...what might ae happened...I couldnae see onythin. But I stared intae the dark. Waitin to see the tail lights again as the train rounded the curve in the bridge as she headed intae Dundee. I didnae see the lights again, but there was nae way

ae tellin...if that was on account of the storm...I just didnae see
onythin...

I waited for a few seconds...then I opened the door and looked oot
but the rain was in ma face...and I couldnae...so I went doon for
some more coals and brought them in for the fire. Like nothing was
wrang...but I had nae wey ae kennin yet. I would only ken...in a few
meenits ...by there bein the sound ae the bell tae let me ken the train
was past the signal cabin at the North end ae the bridge...and the
line was clear...

(He looks at the bell, moments pass....)

But there was nothing. Nae signal. Nae bell. Nae signal came fae the
Northern shore.

I dinna kenn hoo lang I waited...mebbe two and half minutes...
three minutes. I dinna ken why I waited that long...but I was mebbe
afraid...afraid ae lookin foolish...besides we were discouraged fae
using emergency procedures unless we were sure something had
happened...and I wasnae sure...I didnae really ken onythin. It may
no have even been that lang. My mooth was dry.

But eventually I tried my signal. I tried tae ring the signalman ahead
and see if he would answer me. I had two speaking instruments. I
tried them baith n'aa. Nothin. Communication was cut. Aa the lines
were disconnected.

I remember...I felt...Weak. Quite weak...then I collected mysel...I
signalled back tae St Fort that naethin should come through... and I
put ma coat oan... and then I left the cabin...I walked oot ontae the
track.

(Lighting change.)

Absolute black. Darkness. Like death or sleep. But it wasnae silence.
In nae way was it silent. Aa the invisible devils in hell were loose
at wance. And aa shoutin at me. Aa ae them. Bawlin. Wi sudden
shrieks in my face. Harryin my soul.

I strained ma een intae the darkness like if I stared hard enough, my
een might throw light. But I could see naethin. Nae shapes even...I
couldnae even see the clouds that covered the moon. I kennt the
moon was there, the warld was there, the bridge was there. But I
couldnae see ony ae it.

But I could hear, by Christ. I could hear the storm aa roon me, like hell's gate had opened…and I could feel it…the wind, freezin…the rain oan my face and ma hauns…ma troosers…soaked through in an instant…

I could feel ma baws shrink into ma scrotum. I could. Like they were telling me…aw naw…dinna dae this…wir no fer this gemme. Yer oan yer ain, Tommy…

The light ae ma cabin was ahint me…but I threw nae shada afore me. I looked back for a last keek ae the light. Then I put ma heid doon against the wind and walked intae the derk.

Horizontal, black rain. And terrifying wind, hammers ae it, invisible. And cold? You never felt anything the like o it… Like I was naked…blin…droukit…deefened. My face stingin, the wind tuggin at my ears like they were bein ripped aff ma skull. My een hurt like the wind was clawin them oot ae ma face. I had tae close them, there was that much watter lashin at them, at my face, in ma my hair. Closin them made nae difference tae the dark.

I looked ahint me. The light ae ma signalman's cabin was as loast as the line ahead…like I was the only thing alive in the endless black…I felt loast, like a child…that couldnae find its mithers haun in the dark…Aw ae a sudden…aw my experience, aw I'd done wi ma life up tae then, was stript awa by the wind. And the loneliness.

(Acting out his walk.)

I was feelin my way by the sleepers…tappin the side ae ma fit oan yin rail and then the yin the ither side…then ah must ae stepped oot ontae the span itsel, and Christ…if I'd thocht it was windy afore! The wind gustit…and there was a sound fae the wind… like a bark…a laugh…I swear it was like the devil was laughing at me…for a contemptible wee craytur…and he liftit me clear aff ma feet and for wan terrifying instant I was hanging in the air…hanging like a doll in his giant haun…the devil held me up and looked right through me tae my backbone …wi black eyes in a black face in the black desert ae the storm…and he threw me doon…broken and useless. And as I fell, I mind it clearly, screaming in terror…begging that the devil hadnae thrown me fae the bridge intae the water below. That water was death. Instant, clinging death, freezing, weighting, pulling…

yer lungs emptying in a sudden scream, in the sudden silent freezin dark…then nothin.

But no. I landit on the grun…the track…I'd been liftit straight up and back…I was oan my back, grateful for the pain o it, grateful for the wind howling, grateful I'd thrown my hauns oot tae catch the grun…and I'd caught it, cutting ma hauns, scraping the skin aff them, cutting my elbows…ma heid banging…no hard aff the rails… nae too hard…but hard enough for it tae hurt me…and let me ken I was alive…

And I lay there sobbin at ma ain terror, at the shame o it. Weepin, keenin like a beast, but kenning like a man that at least I was safe tae weep…for there was naebiddy tae hear me cryin…Ma tears wad be loast in the rain coursin in rivers doon ma face. As I was lost in the universe…

I was wet, I was cold…I was scared oot ma wits. But I wasnae fuckin deed…And I lay there a moment, acceptin ma helplessness, becoming accustomed tae this universe where I fun masel…this hell…this circle ae hell where the black, freezin rain wuz rippin at my face…where this was the punishment for some sin ae luxury I'd committed, some meal I'd owre eaten…some pleasure I'd enjoyed that by Christ I was peyin fer noo!

And I kennt that if I was tae learn what had happened tae the train, I'd need tae crawl…I'd need tae go oan ma hauns and knees so as not be be blawn owre and intae the river. So…I turned ower on the tracks…

Everythin was still howling, freezing invisibility ahead ae me and behind…I couldnae even see the grun…And I startit crawling. Feeling the rails oan either side ae me, and the sleepers as my hands felt them, and the gravel atween the sleepers…

And I became calm. I made a routine ae it. I coontit. I put nummers against the storm, human reason against the chaos ae nature. Ma ain wee self- contained world…my body, bent and ridiculous, nae doot. But movin, movin in the dark. I had purpose, I had meaning. My humanity was regained by my proper deference tae the storm. By kenning that the wan way tae be safe, as I crawled oot owre the water, the raging water fifty feet ablaw…amid the raging weather aw aboot me…was tae ging oan aw fours like an animal, heid bowed in praise ae the forces greater than any man…that ony man standin up…could deal wi.

And as I went, safe noo…I began thinkin human thoughts. Thoughts aboot the future. Whit the fuck I was deein, like. Practical things like that began tae occur tae me noo ma terror was contained, locked in my crawling limbs…

How lang's the bridge? How lang will it tak me tae crawl this way? I lifted my heed. Still naethin. Nae lights, nae shapes…no even the high girders ae the centre ae the brig…so I kept going…one two three four…one two three four as I moved my limbs. How many sets ae four…one…two…three…four…and how far did I travel wi each set…two feet…one…

And I started tae rebel against masel…like Satan did in heaven… what was I achieving? How could I even tell? This could take hours…and it might be for naethin. What I'd seen…what I thought I'd seen through the windae ae ma cabin…might be naethin…I might be mekkin a fool ae masel, putting masel in herm's wey…fer nothing…when I could be in my warm cabin, where I'd stood up a lifetime ago…stood straight up fae clearing ashes fae the fire… when I'd seen…what I thought I'd seen…the fire…the orange glow ae it…the bone warming heat ae it…the light in my cabin fae the four paraffin lamps I'd left burning… The light…the heat…the safety ae ma cabin…how long had it been? Minutes, hours…since I'd left that safety, that warmth and light and human activity…hours ago I'd startit crawling on this man made spit ae concrete intae this overwhelming, howling darkness…what the hell was I deein?

I had tae stop. I had tae breathe again…slow my breathing…count that too. In…one …two out…one…two…

And restore masel fae being owrewheemed by fear.

I tried tae mind the bridge in day light? How lang was it till I reached the low walls that held the first ae the girders ae the central span. Christ, I didnae even ken! I'd seen it in daylight every working day, six days a week for eighteen months…I'd seen it in the light and sun…and now I couldnae bring onythin I kenned tae mind.

God all fucking mighty! Could I even turn? Could even I turn on this narrow single track?

I went on. Hand owre hand...moving my feet. How many sets ae four...a hundred...two...how far was I out across the bridge. I could still see nothing...

If only I could see,

I'd came outside...I'd left my nice warm cabin...and I'd been lifted and dropped by the devil...and now I was here, hand over hand like a drowned dog...crawling...and tae what? Aye...tae what?

Tae sudden nothingness...if the bridge had collapsed, might I no reach the edge afore I even kenned it...just suddenly, there'd be naethin unner ma haun...and the weight ae ma arm might pull me owre...

and I'd find mysel falling, hearing the waves crash ablaw me invisible and roarin on the wreck ae the carriages...on their bodies...and I'd scream...wi naebiddy tae hear me....

And as I thought ae that....I couldnae move. I just...couldnae go ony further. I tellt my limbs, my arms and legs...tae move. But they wouldnae. I was frozen...

Course I was cold...but this wasnae that...

I was afraid. I was terribly afraid. I was shocked at masel...but it was beyond my will...there was naethin I could dae aboot it. I couldnae underston it...but I was as still as a frozen beast in a field. Awaiting slaughter. Too scared tae run away.

Lighting change. Wind drops. We return to the witness stand, with **BARCLAY** *reliving the trauma of his testimony.*

Why did you not go on?

I could not continue.

You could not continue? How far were you able to get?

Not far. Not so far as I'd thought...

Approximately?

Thirty or forty yards...it had seemed a lot mair oan the wey oot but...I was quickly back.

Do think you could have gone further? Had you persisted?

I might...I couldnae say.

I see. We'll pass on from there...for the moment. What did you do then?

I made my way onto the shore...tae see...if I could see onythin fae there. I thought mebbe I'd see better fae the shore...I went backwards, forwards...tae each side...east and west ae the bridge... tae try and see...I was at the east side...when the moon came oot...and I saw....that the bridge had given way. The moon broke pale white light...on everything...just for a moment...through the clouds...and I saw...I glimpsed...the gap...the remains of the pillars standing up like teeth...monstrous...a mouth....broken...waves smashing on them, frae every side, tearing at them like dogs tearing at a cornered fox...the river overwhelming the work of man...the storm had pulled everything to pieces...it was like seeing the end ae the world...the human world...then darkness fell again...and I saw nothing.

What did you do?

Sorry? Could ye repeat the question?

Seeing that something serious had happened to the bridge...what were your thoughts?

The train...the train I'd sent owre. The driver...the man I kenned... the stoker...who I didnae ken...the boy I'd gien the train staff...I thought ae them...Ae the folk whose faces I'd seen in the paraffin lights ae the third class carriages...I still didnae ken...fer sure if they were in Dundee safe...or not...or if they were in that mouth... if they'd fallen...So I walked...to the station...tae St Fort. They didnae ken onything either. They were shocked. The man Nichol and myself...fae St Fort...We walked thegither to the next...station. Where we were tellt that the train had not arrived in Dundee.

And how did you feel? How did that make you feel?

Pause. Lighting change. Seagulls, a peaceful sea. We return to the 'present.'

There was a chap next day...the day efter I testified. He was dredging for mussels at sunset...on Greenside Scalp...that's aboot three miles north east ae the bridge.

(He tears up.)

He saw something in the watter. Something atween the sand banks and he took his boat oot and he hooked her…and he turned her owre… she was the first yin found…a servant.

The story is that when they took the body back tae the refreshment room at the station that they'd prepared as a mortuary…there were three sisters waiotin there who started screamin the moment the body was laid oot…begging tae see her… see their mother…and eventually, tae shut them up, the railway officials let them through, and the lassies stopped screaming. Cos it wasnae her. They didna ken who it was.

Her name was Annie. It turn toot. Annie Cruikshank. She was a housemaid. Sixty three year old. She worked for a Lady that lived in Moray Place in Edinburgh, wan ae the best addresses in the country…and almost as soon as she'd been identified, the stories startit aboot her…

Annie Cruickshank was a thief, they said…she'd worked faithfully for Lady Baxter for thirty year…but her pockets were full ae silverware she'd stolen fae Moray Place…

She was sixty-three years old…nivver a peep aboot her onywhere in the world…and noo she was a thief. A deed thief.

It was the same when they startit findin ither bodies…there hid tae be a story, never mind if it was true or not…these pair were star crossed lovers…this wan was an anarchist oan his way tae bomb Aberdeen…this was a murderer….

(Angry.)

They couldnae just be folk. They had tae be stories. Nane ae them had tae be true…but we had tae have stories…the stupider the better. Why? Why dee we dee that tae each ither? Why dae we make stuff up? Is life no complicatit enough?

Or is it just the opposite? That we make things simple fer oorsels by fittin ither folk intae the kinda stories we were tellin yin anither onyway. Aboot how everybody fae Fife is like this…and every Frenchman is like this…ur German like that…when just fae kenning oorselves we ken that's rubbish. We'd nivver sanction sic simple mindit nonsense aboot oorsels…why dae we accept it aboot ither folk? Why dae we insist on it?

We must need tae, somethow…it must be something aboot how wir made that means its only possible tae live in a world made ae stupit stories. We cannae live in the real world. And those that shout the loudest aboot how we need tae be realistic, are the stupidest story tellers ae the lot.

God had tae be punishin somebody fer something…somebody had tae be tae blame… It aa had tae mean something. It couldnae just be an accident….and that's where I cam in…ye see? The way they asked me questions…they were lookin somebody…anybody…tae fit intae a story, tae step up and take the blame.

And I awriddy blamed masel…fer sendin the train oan, fer turnin back on the bridgte. I didnae need them tae blame me. I awriddy blamed masel.

And in the end…of course …the enquiry blamed the company for savin money on the metal content ae the rivets…and they blamed the original design ae the bridge by Sir Thomas Bouch…he hadnae reckoned tae the high winds on the high girders…

That the train has struck the metal ae the girders, liftit aff by the wind…that explained the sparks I'd seen…me and a dozen ither witnesses…and the bridge, weakened awriddy, collapsed.

Anyway, Sir Thomas died ae shame…a year later…and somebody else designed then bridge owre the Forth…

I'd shaken his hand wance. Seemed like a nice enough chap.

So I didnae ken how tae feel when it was in aw the papers that he was the story, he was the one tae blame, and he was dead noo so that was an end ae the matter…an end tae thought…and a new bridge ae a new design would rise fae the mooth ae the waters that nivver gave up merr than hauf their dead…

The law held me blameless. And that was that.

But there's a difference between what the law says…and what ye feel. Between what ye know…and what ye feel.

Forty years I've woken up at night reliving it…the guilt…Forty years a signalman…sending signals…meanings…that mean nothing.

Forty years. And this morning…this…

(He takes a telegram from his pocket.)

My grandson...named for me...oot wi his regiment, the Fife and Forfar Yeomanry...who lied aboot his age in 1914...and we aa went alang wi it...thinking it would be over by the time he finished training...and when it wasn't over...feeling sick each day he was oot there...first in Gallipoli, wi the Turks and the plague there... surviving it...surviving day after day the kind ae blind helpless fear that I'd only kennt wance...wan night...then the relief ae him being stationed in Cairo...fighting natives in the Egyptian desert, then surviving the Turks again in Palestine...while we thanked God he wasnae in France or Flanders...and finally he was there last year when the German offensive finally broke the trenches oan the Western Front...and we were so afraid...but him living through all that, keepin aw his postcards ae Cairo and Jerusalem...and this morning a telegram comes...and he's died ae flu...Spanish Flu. In the barracks...at hame in Kirkaldy.

Twenty-two year old. Younger than me when that bloody bridge...

He happened tae be there when the flu everyone thought was over wi last winter, when it came back...like Eliza Smart or Annie Criuikshank or David Neish...just happened tae be on that train that night...just visiting their parents...or just coming back tae work after the weekend...It means nothing, naebiddy chose them... naebiddy punished them...it doesnae mean a bloody thing.

My grandson...came through four year ae the bloodiest war in human history wi oot a bliddy scratch...and died ae flu in Kirkaldy and that means nothing either.

And noo ma faither's name will die wi me...and I never even liked ma faither...sitting there wi his wee red face while the experts were looking for somebody tae blame...

(The bell sounds.)

That means something. That means the line is safe...and clear...and that means I have work tae do...tae send the next train through.

(He puts on his coat.)

It's only when the bell doesnae ring...that's when we stare intae nothingness...that we have tae pretend that there might be something there...tae tell us what it aw means...

(He picks up his lamp.)

As it happens, it's no a bad night for the time ae year.

(He exits. End.)

9 781913 630003